Buttons, Buttons

| Written by Elizabeth Lane | Photographs by Carl Wayne Andreason |

S0-ASC-228

Sometimes, on rainy days,
I get out my button box.

I dump all the buttons on
the table and sort them.

I sort out the big, brown
buttons from Dad's old coat.

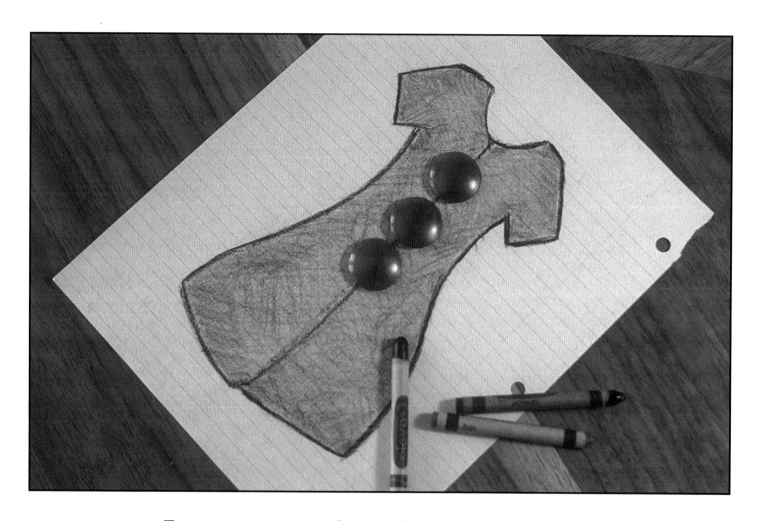

I sort out the shiny, red
buttons from Mom's dress.

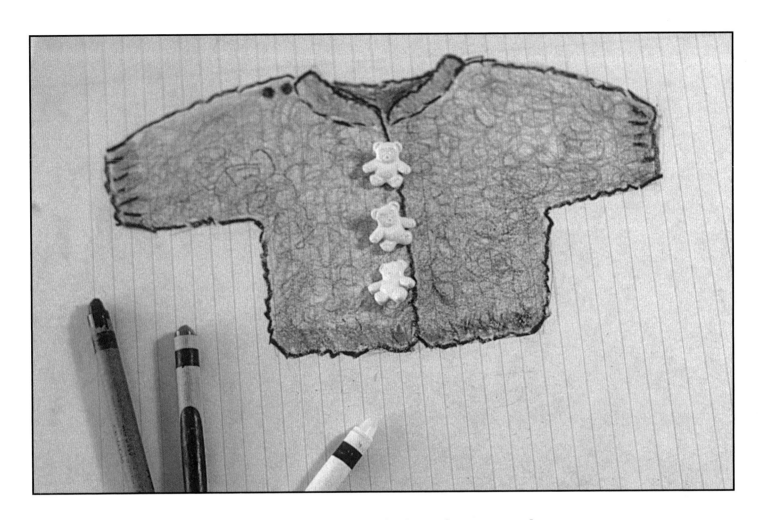

I sort out the teddy-bear buttons
from my old baby sweater . . .

and the eagle buttons from
Uncle Troy's old army jacket.

Next I sort out all the blue
buttons with four holes, . . .

then the white buttons with
two holes.

I sort out the big, black buttons . . .

and the fancy silver buttons.

Then I put them all away
to sort on another rainy day.